iPAD PRO USER'S MANUAL

The Complete Guide to Master iPad Pro and iOS

Daniel McDermott

Copyright © 2019 by Daniel McDermott - All rights reserved.

iPad Pro is a trademark of Apple Inc. all other copyrights & trademarks are the properties of their respective owners, Reproduction of any part of this book without the permission of the copyright owners is illegal-except with the inclusion of brief quotes in a review of the work.

Contents

Introduction 1

How to Set Up Your New iPad Using Automatic Setup 4

How to Send and Receive SMS Messages on iPad and Mac via Text Message Forwarding 8

How to Identify and Remove Unnecessary Apps 11

    How to Reinstall Deleted Apps 13

How to Shut Down or Force Restart 14

How to Take a Screenshot 16

How to Access Control Center and Home Screen in iOS 12 With the iPad's New Gestures 17

How to Use the iPad App Switcher 22

Create and Use Memoji in iOS 12 24

How to Access and Set Up Parental Controls 33

Changes to Notifications in iOS 12 41

Apple Pay Cash 48

How to Take Burst Photos 56

How to Use the Magnifier Feature 59

How to Enable and Disable Critical Alerts in iOS 12 61

How to Recover Files, Contacts, Bookmarks, Calendars and Reminders in iCloud 63

How to Use Instant Notes on iPad With Apple Pencil 67

How to Change the Tap Gesture on the Apple Pencil 2 71

How to Hide Pictures From the Photos App in iOS 12 72

How to Use Safari's Private Browsing Mode and Delete Your Browsing History 75

How to Use iCloud Keychain on Your iOS Devices 80

Getting the Most Out of Your iPad 84

How to Perform a Quick Website Search in Safari 95

How to Drag and Drop Text Between Apps on the iPad 98

How to Change Siri's Voice 100

iii

Introduction

Apple in October 2018 overhauled its iPad Pro lineup, introducing revamped 11 and 12.9-inch tablets that adopt an iPhone XS-style design with an edge-to-edge display, slim bezels, and no Home button.

With no Home button for navigation or biometric authentication, the iPad Pro features a TrueDepth camera system with Face ID to replace Touch ID. Face ID on the iPad Pro works in both portrait and landscape orientation.

The 11-inch model replaces the 10.5-inch iPad Pro, offering more display in a body that's the same size. The new 12.9-inch iPad Pro has the same 12.9-inch display but in a smaller body with 25 percent less volume. Both of the new iPad Pro models are super thin at 5.9mm, with Apple eliminating the headphone jack.

Design wise, the new 11 and 12.9-inch iPad Pro models feature a re-imagined aluminum chassis featuring flat, rounded edges reminiscent of the iPhone SE, which wrap around the new Liquid Retina display. Apple says the new iPad Pro models feature its most advanced display ever with wide color support, True Tone for adjusting to the ambient light, and ProMotion 120Hz refresh technology.

Inside, the 2018 iPad Pro models are equipped with an eight-core A12X Bionic chip that offers 35 percent faster single-core performance and up to a 90 percent boost during multi-threaded tasks compared to previous-generation models. A new seven-core Apple-designed GPU offers twice the graphics performance.

According to Apple, the iPad Pro is faster than 92 percent of all portable PCs, and even with the increased speed, the new models offer all-day 10-hour battery life.

A next-generation Neural Engine is included, offering improved performance for Core ML tasks and augmented reality features. Most of the iPad Pro models feature 4GB RAM, but the higher-capacity 1TB models have 6GB RAM.

Instead of a Lightning port, the new iPad Pro adopts a USB-C port that lets it connect to USB-C accessories including 4K and 5K displays. The USB-C port on the iPad can also be used to charge accessories like the iPhone and Apple Watch.

At the back of the iPad Pro, there's a 12-megapixel f/1.8 aperture camera with Smart HDR, a Quad-LED True Tone Flash, wide color, and support for 4K video recording at up to 60fps. Unlike previous iPad Pro models, the new version does not support optical image stabilization, instead using auto image stabilization.

The front-facing TrueDepth camera features a 7-megapixel lens with support for Portrait Mode, Portrait Lighting, Animoji, Memoji, and Smart HDR. Other iPad Pro features include four speaker audio, five microphones, Bluetooth 5.0, and Gigabit LTE.

The iPad Pro is equipped with a series of magnets that let it connect to a second-generation Apple Pencil that supports tap gestures, simple pairing, and wireless charging. Apple is also selling a new Smart Keyboard Folio alongside the iPad Pro and Apple Pencil 2.

How to Set Up Your New iPad Using Automatic Setup

If you got a new iPad and you already have at least one iOS device that's running iOS 11, setting up the new device is simple and quick with Automatic Setup. Introduced in iOS 11, Automatic Setup streamlines the setup process for new iPhones and iPads, transferring over Apple ID info, your WiFi network credentials, your preferred settings, and your iCloud Keychain.

Automatic Setup is meant to be used in tandem with a restore from an iCloud backup, because while it transfers many settings, it does not offer full device-to-device content transfer. When you buy a new device, Automatic Setup will pop up automatically, but there are some steps to follow to get everything transferred over:

- Power on your new device, which will open up to a menu asking you to pick a language.
- After choosing a language, you'll see a "Set Up Your iPad" prompt.

- When this appears, place your existing iOS device near the new device to initiate Automatic Setup.
- Your existing device will show a pop up letting you know you can use Automatic Setup. Tap "Continue" to start.
- An Apple Watch-style pairing image will appear on the new device, and you'll be instructed to scan it with the camera on your existing device.
- In an area with decent lighting, hold the existing device's camera over the image on the new device to pair the two together.
- Enter the passcode from your existing device on the new device.
- From there, all of your data will start transferring from the old device to the new device.

When the first few Automatic Setup steps are complete, your iPad will walk you through setting up Touch ID/Face ID, Siri, and Apple Pay, which are separate steps.

An additional "Express Settings" feature following Automatic Setup is designed to speed up new device activation even further. Express Setup automatically enables Find My iPad, location services, and analytics, so if you don't want these features on, make sure to tap "Customize Settings" to change them.

Once you've transferred all of your settings with Automatic Setup, you can restore from an iCloud backup to get all of your apps transferred over. If you want to set up a device as new without downloading all of your old content, though, you're finished once Automatic Setup is completed.

If you don't have an iOS device running iOS 11, you'll need to go through a more traditional setup process. The steps are a lot like Automatic Setup, but instead of choosing an existing device after setting a language, you'll need to manually enter data like your Apple ID and your WiFi password.

How to Send and Receive SMS Messages on iPad and Mac via Text Message Forwarding

Ever since iOS 7, Apple has provided a Text Message Forwarding service that can push SMS messages received through your iPhone's cellular network to your other Apple devices.

Using the same network, the forwarding service also allows you to send messages from your iPad or Mac to other phone numbers, even if they don't support Apple's iMessages platform (dumbphones and Android devices, for example).

For whatever reason, the Text Message Forwarding feature may not be enabled on your iPhone, so if you tend to miss standard text messages coming through to your phone when you're engaged with something on your Mac or iPad, it's definitely worth enabling.

Once activated, those messages will show up on all your devices in the Messages app as green chat bubbles, allowing you to distinguish them from regular blue iMessages. To activate the feature in iOS 11:

- Launch the Settings app on your iPad.
- Tap Messages.
- Tap Send & Receive.
- Tap Use your Apple ID for iMessage.
- Tap Sign in to use your Apple ID for iMessage, or tap Select Other Apple ID and then enter the login credentials for the account you want to use.
- Wait for a moment while iMessage activates. Click OK in any dialog boxes that confirm your Apple ID is now being used for iMessage on your other devices.

- Tap back to Settings -> Messages, and tap the new Text Message Forwarding option in the menu.
- Use the toggle buttons next to the devices in the list to include or exclude them from the Text Message Forwarding service. Note that only devices logged into the same iCloud account and connected to the same Wi-Fi network will appear in the list.
- A security code may appear on the devices that you enable – make sure to type the code into your iPad to activate them for the service.

If you followed the steps above but the Text Message Forwarding option doesn't appear in your iPad's settings app, check that your device is connected to Wi-Fi and the internet connection is good.

Another solution is to turn off and then restart iMessages via Settings -> Messages -> iMessage. You can also try signing out of iMessage and signing in again: Select Settings -> Messages -> Send & Receive, tap your Apple ID at the top, and then tap Sign Out.

How to Identify and Remove Unnecessary Apps

With so many paid-for and free apps available on the App Store these days, it's easy to reach a point where you have so many of them on your iPhone or iPad that a sizable proportion are simply forgotten about, and soon storage space starts to become an issue.

Fortunately, there's an easy way that you can keep tabs on which apps you use the most and which ones have basically become redundant to you, and are just adding needless clutter to your home screen and eating up storage. Follow the steps below to learn how it's done.

How to Identify and Delete Redundant iOS Apps

- Launch the Settings app on your iPhone or iPad.
- Tap General.
- Tap iPhone Storage.
- A list of all the apps (including stock apps) on your iOS device will load in order of size, with the largest apps listed first. Scroll down the list and look at the Last Used: date underneath the title of each app. If it's been several weeks or months since you opened an app, or it says Never Used, then consider uninstalling it – tap the app in the list.
- Two uninstall options are presented on the screen. Tap Offload App to unload the app but preserve any documents and data (these are reinstated if you later reinstall the app) or tap Delete App to

remove the app and all related data from your device.

If you tend to download a lot of apps that often get left unused, consider enabling the iPhone Storage menu recommendation to automatically Offload Unused Apps when you're low on storage. If you uninstall a purchased app but later decide that you want to use it (and it's still available in the App Store) simply follow the steps below.

How to Reinstall Deleted Apps

- Launch the App Store app on your iPad.
- Tap the Today tab if it isn't selected already.
- Tap your circular profile photo at the top-right of the Today screen to access the account settings screen.
- Tap Purchased.
- In the Purchased screen, tap the Not on this iPhone/iPad tab.

- Scroll through the list of purchased apps to find the one that you want to reinstate, and tap the cloud download icon next to it to re-download and install.

How to Shut Down or Force Restart

Apple's 2018 iPad Pro models, available in 11 or 12.9-inch size options, feature edge-to-edge displays with no Home buttons included. The lack of a Home button has resulted in some re-mapped gestures and features, with Apple introducing new restart, shut down, and force restart methods in the tablets.

A shut down and a restart are the same gesture now, while a force restart, used if a regular restart won't work, is a bit different. To Shut Down/Restart Your iPad

- Press and hold down on the top button and either the volume up or volume down button until a slider appears.

- Slide a finger along the slider to turn off the iPad.
- Once it's turned off, press and hold on the top button again until the Apple logo appears.

On previous devices, you could restart by holding down the home button and the side button on a device at the same time, but in the new models, you need to do a full shutdown and then power the tablet back up in a separate step. You can also turn off your iPad by opening up the Settings app, choosing General, and selecting "Shut Down." To Force Restart Your iPad:

- Press and quickly release the volume up button.
- Press and quickly release the volume down button.
- Press and hold the Power button until a restart is initiated.

All of the gestures used in the new iPad Pro models are the same as the gestures used in the iPhone X and later, so you can also follow these same steps to shut down or restart an iPhone without a Home button with one small tweak - you'll need to hold the Side button on the right because there is no top power button.

How to Take a Screenshot

Apple's newest iPad Pro models, available in 11 and 12.9 inches, are the first iPads not to feature a Home button. On traditional iPads, you press on the volume button and the home button to take a screenshot.

On the new iPad Pro models, taking a screenshot is just as easy, but the gesture is a bit different. To capture a screenshot, press on the power button located at the top of the device and the volume up button located on the right of the device at the same time.

The two buttons are located closely together, so it's just a quick pinch gesture. This is the same way you take a screenshot on the iPhone X and later, Apple's iPhones without home buttons.

Make sure to press the volume up button and not the volume down button as the volume up + power gesture is the only gesture that will capture a screenshot. Pressing volume down and power will ignore the volume down and turn the display off. You'll also need to make sure just to press and release, as holding down the buttons will initiate a restart.

How to Access Control Center and Home Screen in iOS 12 With the iPad's New Gestures

Apple in iOS 11 revamped the iPad's interface and changed the way we interact with the tablet through a new Dock, a revamped App

Switcher, and Drag and Drop, and with iOS 12, further iPad changes have been implemented.

There are new gestures to learn for accessing the Home screen, App Switcher, and the Control Center, along with a new status bar.

The new iPad gestures are identical to the gestures on the iPhone XS. If you use an iPhone X, XS, or XR, the new iPad gestures will be familiar to you, but if you don't, it could take a bit of time to get used to.

In iOS 11, when you wanted to access the Home screen from within an app, you would press the Touch ID Home button. That's still true, but you can also now get to the Home screen when you swipe up from the bottom of the display.

When in an app, swiping up from the bottom of the screen takes you right to the Home screen rather than just bringing up the iPad Dock within an app.

To get to the Dock to open more than one app for multitasking purposes, you need to do a swipe and a slight hold rather than just a swipe at the bottom inch of the screen while you have an app open already.

The iPad Dock in an app. A quick swipe brings you to the Home screen, but a swipe and a hold brings up the Dock in an app.

If you swipe and hold a bit higher on the screen, you can access the App Switcher on the iPad for quickly swapping between apps or closing apps, which is done with a swipe upwards on an app card. This gesture works both within apps and at the Home screen.

The iOS 12 iPad App Switcher, accessible with a longer swipe and hold on the Dock, either at the Home screen or within an app.

Getting to Control Center

Control Center in iOS 11 was paired with the App Switcher and was accessible by swiping up on the Dock, but that gesture now opens the App Switcher alone without providing access to Control Center.

Getting to Control Center is now done by swiping downwards from the right portion of the status bar, where it displays your battery life and Wi-Fi/Cellular connection.

All other gestures on the iPad remain the same, such as a swipe downwards from the top middle of the display to bring up your notifications and a swipe to the right to get to the Today section for widget access, but there are other iPad improvements worth noting in iOS 12.

iPad Status Bar

The iPad's status bar has been redesigned in iOS 12, and it now resembles the status bar of the iPhone XS. The date and time are listed on the left hand side of the status bar, while battery life and Wi-Fi/Cellular signal and connection are displayed on the right hand side.

The middle of the display, where the date was previously shown, is left open, perhaps for a future notch. Prior to iOS 12, the iPad's status bar did not show the date, so that's also a new addition.

Spacebar Trackpad

When typing on the iPad, if you press and hold with one finger on the space bar, it turns the keyboard into a trackpad to make it easier to navigate through a document and move the cursor.

This is a feature that has been available on iPhones with 3D Touch and on the iPad with two fingers, but in iOS 12, it's simpler to use. A two finger touch also continues to work.

How to Use the iPad App Switcher

On the iPad, iOS 11 and iOS 12 merge the Control Center with the App Switcher as part of an overhauled interface that's meant to put more of a focus on multitasking. The update also adds new ways to access the App Switcher and it brings new, enhanced app switching functionality. To Access the App Switcher:

- On the Home screen, simply swipe up and hold to bring up the App Switcher.
- Within an app, swipe up to bring up the dock and continue the swipe further to access the App Switcher.
- Alternatively, the App Switcher can still be accessed by a double press on the

Home button on iPads with a Home button.

The new App Switcher displays the Control Center options on the right side of the screen, the dock at the bottom of the screen, and your most recently used apps in a tiled view with large icons so you can see exactly what's open. Swipe left and right to see all of the apps you have open and tap to choose one.

When you open two apps at once using multitasking functionality, the app arrangements are preserved in the App Switcher, so you can quickly switch between multiple multitasking windows with a simple swipe and tap.

Closing Apps

There's normally no need to close apps on iOS because Apple manages the device's power needs and keeps apps from using resources when not in use, but if you need to close an app, here's how:

- Bring up the App Switcher.
- Swipe upwards on any app to close it.

As mentioned earlier, the App Switcher is linked to the Control Center. You can change what's displayed in the Control Center portion of the App Switcher by going to Settings --> Control Center --> Customize Controls.

Create and Use Memoji in iOS 12

In iOS 11, Apple introduced animated emoji characters called Animoji, which are designed to mimic your facial expressions. In iOS 12, Animoji have grown to encompass Memoji, which are customizable humanoid Animoji characters that you can design to look just like you.

Memoji can do all of the same things that Animoji can, mimicking your facial expressions to allow for cute videos, photos, and interactions with friends and family. In iOS 12, you can also use Memoji and Animoji in photos through the Messages camera and in live FaceTime chats.

Making a Memoji

- Open up the Messages app.
- Choose a conversation.
- Tap on Animoji Messages app from the Messages app bar, which looks like a little monkey.
- Scroll all the way to the right until you see the "+" button and tap it.

Customizing Your Memoji

Memoji start out as a blank face, and it's up to you to customize it to look like you. The Memoji interface will open up to a display that lets you choose skin tone to begin with. Tapping buttons and sliders will let you customize features and choose options like freckles or no freckles.

To move on from skin tone to other features, tap the labels at the top, cycling through Hairstyle, Head Shape, Eyes, Brows, Nose & Lips, Ears, Facial Hair, Eyewear, and Headwear.

During this entire process, your Memoji is active so you can see what all of the features look like when animated. Sometimes it will pause when changing a feature, but you can resume the animation by tapping on the Memoji.

There are dozens of facial feature options and accessories to choose from when creating a Memoji, allowing for many different looks.

When your Memoji is all finished, just tap "Done" in the upper right hand corner. You can save as many Memoji as you want, so you can make Memoji for yourself, your friends, family, celebrities, characters, and more.

Editing and Deleting Memoji

You can edit an already-created Memoji or delete a Memoji at any time. To do this:

- Open up the Messages app.
- Choose a conversation.
- Tap on the little monkey icon in the Messages app drawer to open up the Animoji Messages app.
- With a Memoji in frame, tap on the three little dots in the left hand corner.
- Choose "Edit" to make changes to your Memoji, choose "Delete" to remove it, or choose "Duplicate" to use it as a base for a new Memoji.

New Animoji Features in iOS 12

In iOS 12, new facial recognition capabilities have been added that let your Animoji and

Memoji mimic both your tongue sticking out and winks. All Animoji and Memoji have tongues, with some special touches like a glitter tongue for the unicorn, a green tongue for the alien, and an articulated tongue for the robot.

Recording a Memoji or Animoji Video in the Messages App

Recording a message, song, or facial expression in a video that can be sent to family and friends is done in the same way that it was done in iOS 11.

With the Animoji app open in Messages and an Animoji or Memoji selected, tap on the red record button to start recording a message. When finished, tap the red stop button, and then tap the blue up arrow to send.

Tapping on the arrow sends the Animoji or Memoji recording automatically to the person you're conversing with.

Using a Memoji or Animoji as a Sticker

Your Memoji and Animoji can also be used as stickers if you just want to send a quick photo reaction but not a full video. To do this, make the desired face and then tap on the Animoji itself rather than the record button to create a quick little screenshot that can be sent using the blue up arrow.

If you want to use the Animoji or Memoji as a sticker to react to another message or to decorate a photo, press a finger on the Animoji and then drag it upwards into the iMessage conversation. While the sticker is attached to your finger, you can use gestures to rotate it and resize it to get the perfect position.

Animoji in the Messages Camera and in FaceTime

iOS 12 includes a new Effects camera in both Messages and FaceTime, which includes support for Animoji and Memoji. You can use Animoji and Memoji to create photos in Messages and to entertain friends and family while in FaceTime conversations.

Animoji in the Messages Camera

- Open the Messages app.
- Choose a conversation.
- Tap on the Camera icon that's next to the iMessage chat bar.
- Tap on the star-shaped icon in the bottom left corner.
- Select the Animoji icon, which looks like a little monkey.
- Choose an Animoji or Memoji and it will pop up over your face.

- After applying an Animoji, tap the small "X" in above the Animoji menu to exit out of the Animoji interface. Your Animoji will still be displayed, but you will also be able to add other camera effects.
- When all of your desired effects are applied, tap the photo button to snap a photo that can then be edited, marked up further, or shared.

With the Messages camera, you can add Animoji, filters, text, shapes, and stickers to your images.

Animoji in FaceTime

- Initiate a FaceTime call.
- After the call has started, tap on the star-shaped Effects icon.
- Choose an Animoji or Memoji, tap it, and it will be displayed over your face.

- As in the Messages Effects camera, tap on the "X" above the Animoji menu and you can also apply other effects while in the FaceTime call.

The person on the other end of the FaceTime call will see the Animoji and any other effects that you have applied, such as filters. You can complement your Animoji FaceTime calls with the aforementioned filters, stickers, text, and all of the other Effects camera options.

Animoji and Memoji only work with the front-facing camera in both Messages and FaceTime, because the TrueDepth camera system is required.

Memoji and Animoji Compatibility

You need a device with a TrueDepth camera system to create Memoji and Animoji, which includes the iPhone X, iPhone XS, and iPhone XS Max. Later, that will also encompass the iPhone XR and upcoming iPad Pro models that are expected to adopt TrueDepth camera systems.

While it's just the iPhone X, XS, and XS Max that can be used to create and display Animoji, others can still see them in FaceTime calls (including Group FaceTime calls) and in photos created with the Messages camera.

How to Access and Set Up Parental Controls

With Screen Time, Apple has introduced a robust set of parental control options in iOS 12, giving parents a way to monitor and limit the amount of time children are spending on their iOS devices, within specific apps, and more.

Screen Time works via Family Sharing, so as long as your children are part of your Family in the Family Sharing settings, you'll be able to view and control their Screen Time options.

Turning Screen Time On

You'll need to turn on and set up Screen Time on all devices owned and used by your children, which is done in the Screen Time section of the Settings app. Here's how to do it:

- Open up the Settings app.
- Navigate to the Screen Time section."
- Choose "Turn on Screen Time."
- When you see the introductory screen asking whether this is your iPad or your child's iPad, select "This is My Child's iPad."

From here, you can choose to set Downtime, which is a set period of time in which your child will be allowed or disallowed from using the iPad, or App Limits, which will restrict certain app categories. At setup, you can also choose Content and Privacy settings, which are further explained below.

If you want to change Downtime and App Limits selections for your child, you will be able to do so at any time by going to the Settings app and selecting Screen Time on the child's device.

A child's Screen Time settings are also accessible on the parent's device for making changes remotely, available by tapping on a child's name in the Screen Time section of the Settings app, listed under the parent's own Screen Time usage.

All of your App Limits, Downtime, and Content Restrictions are protected via a passcode that must be entered to grant more usage time to children when limits have been reached. This also prevents children from changing their own Screen Time settings.

Using Downtime

Downtime sets a schedule that allows you to choose when your child can and cannot use their iPad. You can, for example, choose to restrict access to iOS devices from 10:00 p.m. at bedtime until 7:00 a.m. in the morning, or choose something that limits hours even further, such as during school.

With Downtime, you can opt to block the device at Downtime, which prevents apps from being used entirely sans parental permission or choose for a less restrictive feature that allows children to turn off Downtime themselves or get 15 more minutes of usage before another reminder about Downtime restrictions.

Most parents will likely want to turn on blocking for Downtime to prevent apps from being used entirely, but the non-blocking option is useful for more responsible children where all parents want to do is offer up a reminder that apps shouldn't be used at certain times.

During Downtime, all apps on the iPad are grayed out with little hourglass locks on them, letting children know that time limits have been reached. The exception is certain apps that are always allowed in case of emergency, such as the phone.

Using App Limits

App Limits allow you to finely control how much time your kids spend using certain categories of apps. With App Limits, you can set restrictions on All Apps & Categories, Social Networking, Games, Entertainment, Creativity, Productivity, Education, Reading & Reference, Health & Fitness, and Other.

So, for example, if you want to limit the amount of time a child is spending on Snapchat and mobile games, you can set an

App Limit for those categories for an hour or two.

After the App Limit has been reached, children won't be able to further access those app categories without asking for express parental permission. Apps will be locked with an hourglass symbol and a passcode will be required to enable more time.

As with Downtime, you can set less restrictive rules that serve as more of a reminder by turning off blocking with App Limits.

Always Allowed Apps

With Downtime and App Limits, you can set certain apps to "Always Allowed" to let children access them at all times even when Downtime and App Limits are enabled.

By default, Apple marks Phone, Messages, FaceTime, and Maps as always available apps, but you can select any apps that you want through the Always Allowed app interface, accessible under "Always Allowed" in the Screen Time section of Settings on a child's device.

You can also remove access to all apps, including Messages, with the exception of the phone, which remains available to children in case of emergency.

Always Allowed is ideal if you want your kids to be able to use certain educational or communication apps at anytime while leaving other apps inaccessible.

Selecting Content Restrictions

Apple has always offered Content Restrictions for parents to limit access to music, movies, TV shows, and apps that are inappropriate for younger children, but these parental controls now live under the Screen Time section of the

Settings app alongside the other Screen Time options.

In the Content & Privacy Restrictions section of Screen Time on a child's device, you can do things like limit App Store purchases, prevent kids from deleting apps, disallow access to certain apps, and set age restrictions on entertainment content.

You can also set privacy settings for everything from location to advertising preferences, so, for example, if you wanted to make sure you can always access your child's location, you can turn on Location Services and select Share My Location.

There are even options that prevent children from changing the passcode on their device, restrict account changes, limit volume, and automatically turn on Do Not Disturb While Driving.

Accessing Content & Privacy restrictions requires an adult to input a Content & Privacy passcode, which prevents children from changing these settings.

Changes to Notifications in iOS 12

In iOS 12, Apple has introduced new notification features, providing an expanded set of tools for monitoring and managing notifications in quicker and more intuitive ways.

There have been no changes to the way that Notifications work on the whole, but many of these features make it easier to clear notifications, determine which notifications you want, and make adjustments on the fly.

Grouped Notifications

iPad owners have been asking for the return of grouped notifications for years, and in iOS 12, Apple delivered. Multiple notifications from the same app will be grouped together on the Lock screen of the iPhone, cutting down on clutter. You can tap a set of notifications from a particular app to expand them to see all of the notifications in the list.

You can tap on the "X" next to a notification group to clear all of those notifications at one time, or do the same thing with a swipe to the left.

In the Settings app, you can change the behavior of grouped notifications. Go to Settings > Notifications and tap on any app to see the "Notification Grouping" preferences. Tap that to choose "Automatic," "By App," or "Off" if you'd rather see all of the incoming notifications for a particular app like Messages.

Automatic sorts by app for the most part, but with this setting enabled, you might get two notification groups if you have email threads going with two different people in the Mail app, or multiple conversations in Messages, for example. Or different incoming Messages conversations. By App will make sure all notifications from an app are in one stack, without the sorting that Automatic mode uses.

Instant Tuning

Instant Tuning is a feature that lets you manage a pesky notification right on the Lock screen, giving you the tools to turn notifications for that app off entirely or send notifications right to the Notification Center.

On any notification that's on the Lock screen or in the Notification Center when you swipe down, swipe left on a notification to see settings that include "Manage," "View," and "Clear All."

Select "Manage" from this list to see Instant Tuning options. Notifications set to "Deliver Quietly" will be visible in Notification Center, but you won't see them on the Lock screen, there will be no banner, and there won't be a badge.

To reverse this, tap on a notification from the muted app again, follow the same instructions, and choose "Deliver Prominently." Notification settings can also be changed in the Settings app, also accessible from the Instant Tuning popup. Turn Off, as the name suggests, turns off notifications for that app entirely.

You can also get to your Instant Tuning settings by 3D Touching or long pressing on any notification and selecting the three ellipses.

Note: In iOS 12, Apple will send you alerts asking you if you would like to continue receiving notifications from a particular app if you've been getting a lot of notifications and haven't been interacting with them. When this happens, the alert will feature a "Manage" section so you can access your Instant Tuning settings for that particular app.

Critical Alerts

Critical Alerts are a new type of opt-in notification in iOS 12 that can ignore your Do Not Disturb settings to send important must-see notifications.

These alerts are limited in scope and are available for medical and health related information, home security, and public safety. For example, a person who is diabetic might want to set critical alerts for a glucose monitor when blood sugar is low, so the notification will be delivered even if Do Not Disturb is turned on.

Critical alerts bypass Do Not Disturb and the ringer switch, and will always play a sound. They are meant to be disruptive and for that reason, are going to be highly limited to apps that need these kinds of immediate alerts.

Developers with apps appropriate for critical alerts will need to apply for an entitlement that needs to be approved by Apple. Users will be able to turn off critical alerts on a per app basis separately from other notifications.

Notification Count in Screen Time

Screen Time, Apple's new feature designed to provide you with the tools to monitor when and how you're using your iOS devices, keeps track of all of the notifications that apps are sending you, letting you know which apps are the noisiest.

This information can help you decide if you want to keep notifications turned on for a particular app, or if you might want to mute an app to cut down on interruptions.

You can get to this section of Screen Time by opening the Settings app, choosing Screen Time, selecting "All Devices," and then scrolling down to the bottom. You can see your notifications from the last 24 hours or the last 7 days.

Richer Notifications

In iOS 12, app developers can build notifications that are able to accept user input, so you can interact with notifications in new ways, doing more on the Lock screen without having to open up your iPhone.

With Instagram, as an example, if the app sends you a notification that a friend posted, you might be able to view the photo and then add a like all from the notification.

In this example, you can tap the heart to like the photo, something that wasn't possible in iOS 11. Rich notifications were available in earlier versions of iOS, but Apple has removed the limits that previously restricted interactive touches.

Apple Pay Cash

Apple Pay Cash, Apple's peer-to-peer payments service, became available for developers and public beta testers in the United States with the release of the second iOS 11.2 public beta.

The feature appears to be still rolling out to some users, but most testers who have iOS 11.2 beta 2 installed should be able to access the service. Here's how to use it.

Setting Up Apple Pay Cash

- Open the Wallet app.
- Tap on the Apple Pay Cash card that appears there.

- Apple will walk you through the setup process, and ask if you want to enable Apple Pay.
- You'll be directed to the Settings app to confirm your information. From there, Apple Pay Cash will take a few seconds to activate.
- Once activated, an Apple Pay Cash card will appear in Wallet and you'll be able to access Apple Pay Cash in the Wallet app.

Alternatively, you can also use the Settings app to enable Apple Pay Cash. Go to Settings > Wallet > Apple Pay > Apple Pay Cash and tap the button to toggle it on. Sometimes this option won't show up until it's been activated through the Wallet app.

Sending and Requesting a Payment

- Open a conversation in Messages.
- Tap the Messages App Store icon.
- Choose the "Apple Pay" icon.

- Tap the "+" or "-" buttons to enter an amount, or use the keyboard.
- Tap "Request" or "Pay."
- You'll have an option to preview your payment or request for payment.
- Press the blue arrow button to send.

When sending a payment, the money you've sent will be listed as "pending" in the Wallet app until the person on the receiving end accepts. Once accepted, the payment will be listed in "Last Transaction" under the Apple Pay Cash card in Wallet. While still pending, a payment can be cancelled.

Money that you're sending will be pulled from a linked debit/credit card or from the Apple Pay Cash card itself if you've added funds to that card or received funds from other people. If you send money using the Apple Pay Cash card or a debit card, there's no charge. For a credit card, there's a 3% fee.

When accepting a payment, the cash will be added to your Apple Pay Cash card in the Wallet app. From there, it can be used to make purchases where Apple Pay is accepted like any other card or it can be transferred to a connected bank account.

Apple Pay Cash works in any conversation with a single person. The option won't be available for group messages.

Sending Money via Siri

- Activate Siri.
- Tell Siri to send a payment. Example: "Send $1 to Eric."
- If multiple payment apps are installed, you'll need to confirm that you want to use Apple Pay.
- Unlock your iPad using Face ID or Touch ID.
- Tap "Send."

- Double click the side button to pay on iPhone X or put a finger on the Touch ID Home button to confirm payment on other devices.

Changing Apple Pay Cash Settings

You can access your Apple Pay settings in the Settings app or through the Wallet app.

- Open Settings.
- Go to Wallet and Apple Pay.
- Tap on the "Apple Pay Cash" card.

From this interface, you can add money to your Apple Pay Cash card, transfer your cash to the bank (which requires adding a bank account) and choose to automatically or manually accept payments.

Verify Identity

Once you've sent or received a combined $500 with Apple Pay Cash, you will need to verify your identity. Identity Verification is available in the Settings app, but it may not be fully functional at this time.

- Open Settings.
- Go to Wallet and Apple Pay.
- Tap on the "Apple Pay Cash" card.
- Choose "Verify Identity."

You will be asked to confirm your legal name and address, along with the last four digits of your social security number and date of birth. Apple will also ask questions related to your personal history and request a photo of a driver's license or state ID card.

Once your identity has been verified, you can have up to $20,000 on your Apple Pay Cash card.

Apple Pay Cash Limits

There are limits on the amount of money that you can send per day and per transaction, and the amount of money you can add to your Apple Pay Cash card.

When adding cash, you must add a minimum of $10 per transaction, but you're not able to add more than $3,000. Over a 7-day period, you can add a maximum of $10,000 to your Apple Pay Cash card.

When sending or receiving money, you can send/receive a minimum of $1 and a maximum of $3,000. Over the course of a 7-day period, you can send/receive up to $10,000.

Transferring money to your bank can be done at any time. A minimum of $1 can be transferred at a time or less than a $1 if your total balance is under $1. Up to $3,000 can be transferred in a single transfer, and over 7 days, you can transfer up to $20,000 to your bank account from Apple Pay Cash.

Beta Requirements

To use Apple Pay Cash, the following requirements must be met:

- Both parties must be running iOS 11.2 beta 2.
- An iPad Pro, iPhone 6 or later must be used.
- Two-factor authentication must be turned on.
- You must be at least 18 years old.
- You must be in the United States with a U.S. credit/debit card and social security number if verification is required.
- An eligible credit or debit card must be available in Wallet.

Along with iPhones and iPads running iOS 11.2 beta 2, Apple Pay Cash can also be used on the Apple Watch on devices that are running the second watchOS 4.2 beta. Sending money from an Apple Watch follows the same general process as the iPhone, with payments made and received through the Messages app.

How to Take Burst Photos

Burst Mode refers to when the camera on your iOS device captures a series of photos in rapid succession, at a rate of ten frames per second. It's a great way to shoot an action scene or an unexpected event, since you're always more likely to end up with the picture you were aiming for.

To take a photo in Burst Mode, launch the Camera app from the Lock Screen – if your device is unlocked, select the Camera app from the Home screen or slide the Control Center into view and launch it from there. Once you have a shot in frame, tap and hold the shutter button at the bottom of the Camera interface for the duration of the scene that you're trying to capture.

Notice the counter increase at the bottom of the frame for as long as you hold down the shutter. This indicates how many shots are being captured in the current burst. Simply take your finger off the shutter when you want to end the burst of shots.

When you take a series of burst photos, they automatically appear in the Photo app under the Album name Bursts. You'll also find them in your main Photo Library as well as the Moments section found in the Photos tab. Here's how to view your burst photos and pick out the best images from them for safe keeping.

- Launch the Photos app.
- Tap a collection of burst photos – they appear in the Photos Library as a single picture, but if you look closely, you'll see more images stacked underneath the top thumbnail image.

- Tap Select at the bottom of the screen.
- Swipe the film strip-like ribbon of images below the photo to view the other shots in the burst.

Any dots you see below images in a burst indicate that Apple's algorithms think they have the best focus and detail in the set, but of course you may think differently.

How to Save Individual Images in Burst Photos

- Tap a stack of burst photos in your Photo Library.
- Tap Select in the top-right corner of the screen.
- Tap each image in the series that you want to keep.
- Tap Done in the top-right corner of the screen.
- To keep only the images that you ticked in the burst series, tap Keep Only

Favorites. Otherwise, tap Keep everything.

How to Use the Magnifier Feature

Apple includes an accessibility feature in iOS that's useful if you have a visual impairment, but can even come in handy if your eyes are simply tired or you're struggling to read something like small print, especially in poor light.

It's called the Magnifier, and has several advantages over just opening up the camera app and zooming in to get a better look at something. Enabling it is easy: Launch the Settings app on your iPhone or iPad, navigate to General -> Accessibility -> Magnifier, and toggle on the Magnifier switch.

After that, all you need to do to use it is triple-click the Side button (or Home button, depending on your device). You can also add it to the Control Center by going to Settings -> Control Center -> Customize Controls, and tapping the green plus button next to Magnifier.

When you launch Magnifier, you'll see a camera-like interface at the bottom of the screen, but with some unique features. The slider controls the magnification of the scene in the lens frame, while the button at the bottom left turns on the flashlight so you can illuminate it. The padlock button next to that locks the focus.

Tapping the big button in the center freezes the image (a frozen image is indicated by a yellow ring around the button), allowing you to move your phone around freely and still look at the image. You can also use the magnification slider to zoom in and out of the frozen image.

Note that when you freeze an image in the Magnifier, it isn't saved to your photo album. But if you want to save the entire image, you can. Simply tap and hold on the frozen picture and select Save Image from the contextual popup menu. You'll find a Share option in there, too.

Over on the far right of the Magnifier interface is a button made up of three circles that provides access to additional sliders for adjusting brightness and contrast.

If you suffer from color blindness or another visual impairment, you can swipe through several color schemes in this extended menu and even invert the colors to find which combination works for you.

How to Enable and Disable Critical Alerts in iOS 12

In iOS 12, Apple added several new ways for users to control how and when they receive app notifications, including the ability to group notifications and change their behavior on the fly with Instant Tuning. A lesser known feature in this subset of options is called Critical Alerts. So what are they exactly?

The idea behind Critical Alerts is that if specific apps have crucial information that shouldn't be ignored – notifications related to health, home security, or public safety, for example – then you'll be alerted regardless of your other device settings.

To that end, Critical Alerts override the Do Not Disturb feature if you have it enabled on your iPhone or iPad, and will even arrive with an audio alert when your device is muted.

Naturally, the Critical Alerts feature is going to have limited use – you'd only want appropriate apps to have access to it (think glucose monitoring or weather warning apps) which is why Apple requires that developers apply for an entitlement to support them.

For that reason, there aren't a whole lot of apps that support these alerts just yet, but if you do come across one that advertises Critical Alerts, you still get to choose whether to enable them or not. Here's how:

- Launch the Settings app on your iPhone or iPad.
- Tap Notifications.
- Select the app from the list that you want to enable/disable Critical Alerts for.
- Toggle the Critical Alerts switch on/off.

How to Recover Files, Contacts, Bookmarks, Calendars and Reminders in iCloud

Apple has little known iCloud tools that are designed to let you recover files that have been deleted from iCloud, as well as recover Contacts, Calendars, and Reminders that have been lost.

Lost iCloud data isn't a situation that comes up often, but these tools were introduced following an iCloud Drive bug in 2015 that caused some users to lose documents stored in iCloud Drive, prompting the creation of the tool.

Accessing Your Files on iCloud.com

- Visit the iCloud.com website on your web browser of choice.
- Enter your Apple ID, password, and two-factor authentication code if the feature is enabled.
- Once logged in, click on the "Settings" app in the main iCloud menu.
- Scroll down to the bottom of the page until you reach the "Advanced" section.
- Click on the content that you need to restore. Options include files stored in iCloud Drive, a list of contacts, your

Calendars and Reminders, or your Bookmarks.

Restoring Files

Using the "Restore Files" option on iCloud.com brings up a list of all files that have been deleted over the past 30 days. It includes files from apps that support iCloud Drive, such as Pixelmator, Napkin, and Byword.

You can select a single file to restore or multiple files, should there have been a catastrophic event that caused iCloud Drive to be wiped entirely. Check the box to make a selection and click "Restore File." Using the file restoration tool returns the file in question to iCloud Drive in its original parent folder, much like un-deleting a photo on iOS.

Deleted iCloud Drive files remain available in iCloud for 30 days before being permanently deleted, at which point they become unrecoverable. As a side note, you cannot do a manual permanent deletion with iCloud Drive files as you can do with Photos on iOS - they're sticking around for the full 30 days.

Restoring Contacts, Calendars, and Reminders

Apple regularly archives a list of Contacts, which can be restored to an iOS device at any time. Restoring a list of contacts from the archive will replace the contacts on all iOS devices connected to your iCloud account, while archiving the current list of contacts to ensure nothing is lost. Contacts can't be restored one by one -- this is an all or nothing batch operation.

Restoring Calendars and Reminders works like restoring Contacts. Apple frequently creates a backup for the two apps, capturing snapshots for more than a month. Any of these archives can be used to replace a current Calendar or

Reminder list, replacing the existing information on all connected iOS devices.

Restoring a Calendar will remove all sharing information, so Calendars and Reminders shared with friends and family will need to be shared again. All scheduled events will also be cancelled and recreated, reissuing all invitations for events.

Restoring Bookmarks

Along with Contacts and Calendars, Apple backs up the bookmarks that you have removed from your Bookmarks list in Safari on a regular basis.

To restore them, simply choose the deleted bookmarks you would like to put back in place and then choose the "Restore" option.

How to Use Instant Notes on iPad With Apple Pencil

If you have an iPad Pro, there's a new feature in iOS 11 that's designed to let you open up a new document in Notes just by tapping the Apple Pencil on the iPad's display.

The feature, Instant Notes, works even when the iPad is locked, so you can pick up the iPad and get right to writing without having to go through the hassle of unlocking the device, opening the Notes app, and creating a document.

Using Instant Notes

- On a locked iPad, press the Home button or the sleep/wake button to activate the display.
- Tap the Apple Pencil anywhere on the iPad's screen.
- Once you've tapped the Apple Pencil on the display of a locked iPad, it launches straight into the Notes app, creating a new note for you (or allowing you to edit an existing note, depending on your settings).

Because the iPad is still locked when the Instant Notes Apple Pencil gesture is used, you can't access additional notes or any other apps until you unlock the device with Touch ID. In this locked mode, you can access all of the Notes features, including the pen tools, the document scanner, the camera, and the sketch tools.

Instant Notes can only be activated from the Lock screen on the iPad. When the iPad is unlocked, you'll need to access your Notes through the app or through the new Notes option in the Control Center.

Turning Off Instant Notes

If you don't want to allow the Apple Pencil to open the Notes app, you can turn off Instant Notes in the Settings app.

- Open the Settings app.
- Scroll down to Notes and tap it.

- Choose "Access Notes from Lock Screen." The feature is toggled on by default.
- Select "Off."

Adjusting Instant Notes Settings

You can also adjust your Instant Notes options in the Settings app. A tap with the Apple Pencil can be set to create a new note, resume the last note created on the Lock screen, or resume the last note viewed in the Notes app.

When using the two options to resume the last note created on the Lock screen or in the Notes app, you can also set time limits. For the "Resume Last Note Created on Lock Screen" option, you can choose to automatically create a new note instead of resuming after a set time period.

For the "Resume Last Note Viewed in Notes App" option, you can set a time limit after which a passcode will be required to view the note. This makes sure someone who gets a hold of your iPad can't access sensitive data.

An Apple Pencil is required to activate Instant Notes, so it only works with iPad Pro models including the 9.7-inch iPad Pro, the 10.5-inch iPad Pro, and the 12.9-inch iPad Pro.

How to Change the Tap Gesture on the Apple Pencil 2

To go with the new 11 and 12.9-inch iPad Pro models, Apple designed a second-generation Apple Pencil. In addition to doing away with the Lightning connector thanks to a new built-in magnetic charging method, the Apple Pencil 2 also supports tap gestures.

Tap gestures can be used to do things like swap between a drawing tool and an eraser in a sketching app, which is a super handy way to switch between two tools quickly. You can customize the settings of your Apple Pencil 2 on your iPad. Here's how:

- Open up the Settings app on the iPad with the Apple Pencil connected.
- Choose the "Apple Pencil" section.
- Select the function you want the tap gesture to have.

You can choose between three options for the tap gesture on the Apple Pencil: Switch Between Current Tool and Eraser, Switch Between Current Tool and Last Used, and Show Color Palette. You can also choose to turn the tap feature off entirely if it's not useful.

How to Hide Pictures From the Photos App in iOS 12

Sometimes you might not want certain pictures shot on your iPhone or iPad to take pride of place in your Photo Library, but for whatever reason, you don't want to just outright delete them. Fortunately, Apple's Photos app includes an option to hide certain photos from the main library. This article shows you how.

Bear in mind that hiding pictures via the following method ensures they won't appear in the Photos or For You sections of the Photos app, but they will still be accessible in the Albums section. If you're looking for a more secure way to squirrel away pictures, consider using a third-party app like Safe Lock instead.

How to Hide Pictures in the Photos App

- Launch the Photos app on your iPhone or iPad.
- Tap Select in the top-right corner of the screen.
- Tap the pictures you want to hide.

- Tap the Share button in the bottom-left corner of the screen. (It looks like a square with an arrow pointing out.)
- In the Share Sheet's bottom row of available actions, tap Hide.
- Tap the prompt that appears at the bottom of the screen to confirm.

Note that pictures you choose to hide from your photo library are stored in an album called Hidden, which lives in the Albums tab.

How to Unhide Pictures in the Photos App

- Launch the Photos app on your iPhone or iPad.
- Tap the Albums tab at the bottom of the screen.
- Scroll to the bottom and under Other Albums, tap Hidden.
- Tap Select in the top-right corner of the screen.
- Tap the pictures you want to unhide.

- Tap the Share button at the bottom-left corner of the screen.
- In the Share Sheet's bottom row of available actions, tap Unhide.

How to Use Safari's Private Browsing Mode and Delete Your Browsing History

This section explains how to use Safari's Private Browsing mode, which prevents your browsing history from being logged on your Apple devices. It's a useful feature if you're buying gifts online for friends or family, for instance, and you don't want anyone with access to your devices to find out what you're up to.

Of course, if you've already been browsing where you shouldn't have and didn't use Safari's dedicated privacy mode, don't worry – we'll also show you two different ways of deleting your existing browsing history. Keep reading to find out how.

Using Safari's Private Browsing Mode

Enabling Private Browsing limits Safari in three important ways: It prevents the browser from creating a history of the pages you visit, it stops AutoFill information like website usernames and passwords from being remembered, and any tabs you open won't be stored in iCloud.

Also, for added peace of mind when you browse privately, Safari automatically prevents cross-site tracking, and requests that sites and third-party content providers don't track you as a rule. Additionally, the privacy mode stops sites from modifying any information stored on your iOS device, and deletes cookies when you close the associated tab. To enable Private Browsing in Safari, follow these steps.

- Open Safari on your iPhone or iPad, tap the Pages icon (consisting of two

squares) to bring up the open tabs view, and then tap "Private". Notice how the interface turns a dark gray.
- Tap the "+" icon to open a private tab.
- When you're done browsing, return to the open tabs view, individually swipe any open tabs to close them, and then tap "Private" again. Your private browsing session is now cleared from memory.

Clearing Existing Browsing History

When you clear your browsing history on a device running iOS 11 or higher, the same logs are cleared on any other devices signed into your iCloud account. The following methods also clear all cookies and web data on the device you're currently using, although AutoFill information remains unchanged.

Method 1

The first method outlined below allows you to either limit the clearing of history, cookies and website data to a specific timeframe, or to delete your existing web history altogether.

- Open Safari and with a tab open, tap the Bookmarks icon (the open book) located at the bottom of the screen.
- Tap the tab at the top of the screen with a clock symbol, and you'll see a history of your browsing activity.
- To remove instances of recorded visits to specific web pages, swipe leftwards across individual logs in the list and tap the red delete button that appears.
- To delete the entire browsing history list, tap "Clear" and select the option you prefer from the following: The last hour; Today; Today and yesterday; and All time.

Method 2

The second method of wiping your browsing history might be considered the 'nuke' option, since it clears all history, cookies and website data on that device, regardless of when the sites were accessed.

- Open the Settings app and scroll down to Safari in the list.
- Tap the "Clear History and Website Data" option near the bottom of the menu. (Note that this setting might be grayed out if there's already no history to clear or if parental controls are set for websites.)
- Tap "Clear History and Data" in the popup overlay.

And that's it. Note that these built-in Safari features only make you safer from discovery by other people in the same household.

If your privacy concerns extend to a desire for enhanced security and anonymity online, consider subscribing to a Virtual Private Network (VPN) service that offers an iOS client or supports OpenVPN (Private Internet Access and ProtonVPN are two popular options), and using a Tor-powered browser for iOS.

How to Use iCloud Keychain on Your iOS Devices

iCloud Keychain is a feature of your Apple account that you can use to keep your website login credentials, personal details, credit card details, and wireless network information up to date and available across all your Apple devices.

With so many usernames and passwords to remember these days, iCloud Keychain provides a convenient way of always having this information at hand. And with its AutoFill feature, iCloud Keychain can even enter your credentials for you when required.

It's also very secure, thanks to Apple's use of end-to-end encryption. This means that only you can access your information, and only on devices where you're signed in to iCloud.

How to Enable iCloud Keychain on Your iPhone or iPad

- Open the Settings app and tap your Apple ID banner at the top of the Settings menu.
- Tap iCloud.
- Scroll down the list and select Keychain.
- Toggle on the iCloud Keychain switch and enter your Apple ID password if prompted.

If this is the first time you've enabled iCloud Keychain, you'll be asked to create an iCloud Security Code or use your existing device passcode. You'll also need to enter a phone number where you can receive SMS messages for authorization purposes. If you've already enabled iCloud Keychain in the past, you'll be prompted to enter the passcode that was used to set it up previously.

Accessing Your Login Details in iCloud Keychain

With iCloud Keychain enabled, Apple's Autofill feature will fill in your login credentials for you whenever you come across the relevant input fields on a website or in an app. On occasion, you may encounter a login screen that doesn't play nice with Autofill. In such cases, you'll need to copy and paste your username and password manually. Here's how it's done:

- Open the Settings app on your iOS device.
- Tap Accounts and Passwords.
- Tap App & Website Passwords and use Touch ID if prompted.
- Tap the relevant login entry in the list, or using the search field at the top of the

Passwords screen, type in the name of the app or website for which you need login credentials.

- Long press on the username/password and tap the Copy pop-up option.
- Now navigate back to the relevant app or website, long press the username/password input field, and then tap the Paste pop-up option.

Note that you can delete login credentials by tapping Edit at the top right of the Passwords screen. You can also tap a website entry and use the Edit option to change existing username and password fields.

Adding Credit Cards and Personal Information

You can add personal information and credit card information to iCloud Keychain at any time using your iPad, after which it will be available across all of your devices. Simply follow these steps:

- Open the Settings app.
- Tap Safari.
- Tap AutoFill.
- To add personal information, tap My Info and select your contact card from the list of contacts. To add credit card details, tap Saved Credit Cards and then tap Add Credit Card.

Getting the Most Out of Your iPad

Apple Pencil

Apple Pencil support is the major new feature in the sixth-generation iPad, and there are a ton of useful tricks you need to know if you're new to the accessory.

- Pairing

Pairing the Apple Pencil to the iPad is as simple as uncapping it and plugging the

Lightning connector into the Lightning port on your iPad. You'll see a popup that asks you to confirm to pair, and once you accept, the Apple Pencil is successfully connected to the iPad.

- Charging and Battery

When you connect your Apple Pencil to your iPad, it'll let you know the battery level. You can also check using widgets accessed by swiping to the right of the Home screen. Scroll down to the "Batteries" section where your iPad and its connected devices (including Apple Pencil) are listed.

Don't see a battery widget? Tap on "Edit" at the bottom of the list and tap on the "+" icon next to the "Batteries" option.

The Apple Pencil's battery lasts for approximately 12 hours, and it charges through the Lightning connector on the iPad or with any Lightning cable using an adapter that ships with the accessory.

If your battery is dead and you need your Apple Pencil in a hurry, just plug it in for 15 seconds. That'll get you enough juice to use it for a half hour, so it's never out of power when you need it.

Apple Pencil Capabilities

The Apple Pencil is a sophisticated device that does quite a lot when paired with the sixth-generation iPad. A new touch sensor in the iPad allows for the Apple Pencil to work, enabling a lag-free writing and drawing experience that's identical to using the Apple Pencil on the more expensive iPad Pro.

Your iPad knows when you're using your Apple Pencil and it blocks out other touch input. That means there's built-in palm rejection, so feel free to rest your hand on the iPad while you write or sketch.

There are pressure and positioning sensors included in the Apple Pencil, which let it detect a range of forces to enable pressure-sensitive drawing and writing in supported apps. When you press lightly, you'll get a thin line. Press harder, and you'll get a thicker line.

On the same note, there are two tilt sensors that determine the orientation and angle of the Apple Pencil while you're holding it, a feature that lets you add shading to drawings and sketches by using the side of the tip.

Replacing the Tip

The Apple Pencil has a replaceable tip, so when it wears down, you can swap in a new one. An extra tip comes with the Apple Pencil, and you can purchase an additional package of four from Apple for $19.99.

How often you'll need to change the tip will depend on how much you're using the Apple Pencil, but on average, a tip should last for multiple months to a year or more. To swap it out, turn the tip counterclockwise to unscrew it and then screw on a new one.

Apple Pencil Apps

The Apple Pencil is ideal for taking notes, writing, sketching, drawing, and other similar tasks on the iPad, and because it's been around for several years now, there are tons of apps that offer full support for the Apple Pencil's features. We've listed some of our favorites below:

- GoodNotes 4 ($7.99) - GoodNotes 4 is a comprehensive note-taking app that offers a range of writing and sketching tools, along with OCR for searching through your written notes. You can also use it to annotate documents and PDFs with the Apple Pencil.

- Notability ($9.99) - Notability is another app that offers all of the features you need for taking detailed, concise notes with the Apple Pencil. It's simple, easy to use, and offers tons of writing and sketching tools, but it's not quite as feature rich as GoodNotes 4.
- PDF Expert ($9.99) - If you're going to be editing and annotating a lot of PDFs, it may be worth investing in PDF expert.
- Pigment (Free) - Pigment is a coloring book app that lets you color in intricate designs using the Apple Pencil. Kids love it, and it's relaxing for adults too.
- Affinity Photo ($19.99) - Affinity Photo is a lot like Photoshop - you can use it for drawing, sketching, editing photos, and more. It has full support for Apple Pencil, including pressure sensitivity and

tilt. Use it to apply editing effects to photos or create paintings with its extensive brush library and brush tools.
- Procreate ($9.99) - For sketching and drawing on the iPad, you won't go wrong with Procreate, an app that many iPad artists prefer. Procreate supports high-definition canvases, offers tons of brushes, and has full support for Apple Pencil.

Tracing Through Paper

Want to digitize a drawing that's on traditional paper? The Apple Pencil works through paper, so just place the sheet over the iPad's display, where it will be illuminated by the screen, and then trace the design in your favorite sketching app.

Other Apple Pencil Tidbits

Apple Pencil support is built into apps throughout the iOS 11 operating system. Inline Apple Pencil drawings, for example, can be inserted into Notes and Mail, while a useful Instant Notes feature lets you tap your Apple Pencil on the display of the iPad to automatically open a new note in the Notes app without having to unlock the iPad or manually open the app.

If you use the document scanner in the Notes app to scan a piece of paper, you can then sign it or annotate it with Apple Pencil. It's a useful feature for documents that you need to sign and return to someone. You can also sign standard PDFs, either in the Mail app or right in the Files app.

With the sixth-generation iPad, Apple also added Apple Pencil support to all of its iWork apps, so you can use Apple Pencil with Pages, Keynote, and Numbers. You can also use the

Apple Pencil for drawing on and annotating screenshots and photos with Instant Markup, a feature available in the Photos app or whenever you take a screenshot (just tap on the screenshot icon in the lower left corner).

The Apple Pencil is, of course, designed for note taking and sketching, but you can also use it for navigation just like your finger.

Augmented Reality

The sixth-generation iPad includes an A10 Fusion chip, and while it's not as speedy as the A10X Fusion in the iPad Pro, it's still able to run any app or game in the App Store. Apple specifically said the more powerful A10 Fusion, which was first introduced in the iPhone 7, was added to the sixth-generation iPad to support augmented reality content.

There are now tons of augmented reality apps built using ARKit in the App Store, and you can download everything from Pokémon Go to apps that let you preview furniture to educational apps, all of which have AR content. In the iOS App Store, you'll want to check out the specific AR categories in the apps and games sections.

iOS 11 on the iPad

iOS 11 introduced a whole slew of iPad-specific features that make using an iPad as a computer replacement a much more pleasing experience. The new sixth-generation iPad, with its A10 Fusion processor, supports all of these features.

A persistent dock, for example, houses all of your apps and makes it easier to use the built-in multitasking features for accessing two apps side by side. Using simple drag gestures that are easy to learn, you can use multiple apps in a variety of ways with Slide Over and Split View arrangements.

Picture-in-picture, another multitasking feature in iOS 11, lets you watch a video on YouTube or another source while continuing to use other apps, which is super handy, and drag and drop features make it simple to move files and content from one app to another.

Control Center has been merged with a useful new App Switcher, accessible by swiping up from the bottom of the iPad. With the App Switcher, you can access all Control Center options and quickly switch between open apps with just a tap.

Adding Accessories

While the new iPad supports the Apple Pencil, it doesn't have a Smart Connector and there's no option for a Smart Keyboard. Bluetooth keyboards are supported, though, and if you want to use your iPad for writing, coding, or other keyboard intensive tasks, it's worth picking one up.

The sixth-generation iPad's design is the same as the fifth-generation iPad's design, so all existing iPad keyboards will work with the new model, and there are tons of options out there. Brydge, for example, makes a highly rated $99 iPad keyboard, and there are multiple options from Logitech, like the $99 Slim Folio. You can also use Apple's own Magic Keyboard for a Mac-like typing experience.

How to Perform a Quick Website Search in Safari

There are several ways to search the web in Apple's Safari browser. In this article, we're going to highlight a way of searching specific websites using a lesser-known Safari feature called Quick Website Search. The option is designed to work with sites that have a built-in search field. Here's how it works.

Let's say you want to look up articles on Google that mention device benchmarks. You might do this by typing "Google benchmarks" into Safari's address bar to get results from whichever search engine the browser is configured to use. If you're a bit more search savvy, you might even type "site: nameofthewebsite.com benchmarks" to limit the search to the name of the website. But ideally you'd just navigate to "nameofthewebsite.com" and use the search field provided at the top of the page.

If you take the latter option and Quick Website Search is enabled, Safari will remember that you've used the name of the website search field and offer to use it again in future searches that include the website's name. For example, if you typed "techbooks" followed by "deals" directly into Safari's address bar, you could tap the option Search techbooks.com for "deals" in the suggestions box, and you'd get instant results from techbooks' own on-site search function.

How to Enable Quick Website Search in iOS

The functionality of Quick Website Search depends on how a given site implements its search field, but we've found that it works with most popular websites that offer them, so it's worth making sure you have the feature enabled. To do this on iPad, launch the Settings app, tap Safari -> Quick Website Search and slide the Quick Website Search toggle to the green ON position.

Notice on this screen that you can also tap Edit to remove websites from the list of shortcuts that Safari automatically adds to whenever you use a site-specific search field.

How to Enable Quick Website Search on Mac

The feature works the same way in Safari for macOS. To see if it's enabled, select Safari ->

Preferences... from the menu bar, choose the Search tab, and make sure the checkbox is ticked next to Enable Quick Website Search.

Lastly, if you click the Manage Websites... button next to the checkbox, you can view Safari's list of website shortcuts, remove individual websites, or clear the list completely.

How to Drag and Drop Text Between Apps on the iPad

iOS 11 introduced handy new drag and drop features on the iPad, that let you drag photos, files, links, and more between apps. What you might not know, though, is that drag and drop also works for blocks of text.

Instead of copying and pasting text on the iPad, you can select a block of text and then drag it right into another app using the drag and drop features. Here's how:

- Select a line or paragraph of text, making sure it's highlighted.
- Hold a finger on the highlighted text until it pops off the page.
- Drag the resulting text bubble into a new app.

In apps like Messages, where you can't highlight text, all you need to do is hold down and drag, skipping the selection step.

In addition to moving text between apps, drag and drop is also useful for copying and rearranging blocks of texts within a single app, like Notes or Pages.

You can also use this drag and drop feature with text on the iPhone, but only within the same app, rather than between two apps. The procedure on the iPhone is the same: simply select text and then hold down until it pops up into a little bubble that can be moved elsewhere within the app.

How to Change Siri's Voice

In the United States, the default Siri voice is an American female voice, but if you've never delved into Siri's settings you might not know that you can change that voice to something else that you might prefer more.

- Open up the Settings app on iPad.
- Select "Siri & Search."
- Choose "Siri Voice."
- Tap an option to hear an audio demonstration of what the voice sounds like.
- Leave the option checked to select it and exit out of the Settings app.

These settings are available in all countries where Siri can be used, but not all options may be available in all countries. The voices you have access to will depend on where you live and the language your iOS device is set to.

In the United States with an iPad set to the English language, you can choose from an American, Australian, or British accent in either a male or a female voice.

If you use Siri on a Mac, you can also change the voice there. Just open up System Preferences, choose the Siri option, and use the dropdown menu under "Siri Voice" to choose something new.

I believe you have been able to achieve some tips in this book that has helped you to master your iPad Pro. Thank you for purchasing this book. God Bless You!

Printed in Great Britain
by Amazon